SMART PEOPLE SWEAR

The Ultimate Guide for Unf*cking Your Head to Unleash Healing, Growth and Great Success!

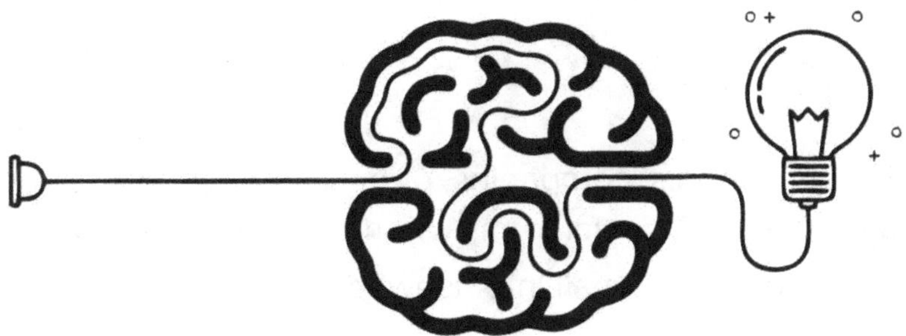

AMY VANDAGRIFF

Smart People Swear (by this workbook): The Ultimate Guide for Unf*cking Your Head to Unleash Healing, Growth and Great Success

Published by Elsewhere Inc.

Wellington, Florida, U.S.A.

Library of Congress Control Number: 2022903273

VANDAGRIFF, AMY, Author
SMART PEOPLE SWEAR
AMY VANDAGRIFF

ISBN: 979-8-9857491-0-6, 979-8-9857491-2-0 (paperback)
ISBN: 979-8-9857491-1-3 (digital)

SELF-HELP / Motivational & Inspirational
EDUCATION / Aims & Objectives

ELSEWHERE
INC.

HAVING A SECURE, ORGANIZED, AND MOST IMPORTANTLY
FOCUSED MINDSET MEANS FINALLY ACHIEVING THE SUCCESS
IN ALL AREAS OF LIFE YOU HAVE BEEN DESIRING

THIS IS NOT THE AVERAGE WORK BOOK, GUIDE BOOK OR JOURNAL

TAKE YOURSELF DEEPER INTO KNOWING

"You see, for all of life is an act of faith and also an act of gamble. The moment you take a step, you do so on an act of faith because you do not see that the floor will remain beneath your feet. The moment you take the journey, what an act of faith. When you enter into any human experience, an undertaking, a relationship, what an act of faith."

-Alan Watts

TABLE OF CONTENTS

YOU ARE HERE 

Welcome to the access control room!

You have found your way back to the master computer control room of your thoughts, beliefs, behaviors, values and even your identity. It may feel as though it has been a while since you have been here, and that is okay.

Sometimes we all feel distanced from our true selves, disconnected even. Making our way back is sometimes an incredible journey to progress from here. The key to all of this knowledge and understanding is about the present moment and the entire journey itself. In a way, it is learning to love every single aspect of it all - the good, bad, ugly and otherwise.

It is how we **DECIDE** to handle things and ourselves and others that ultimately make up the journeys themselves. From a dissociated viewpoint up above and looking down below, we get a seat to watch life itself unfold. Safe and able to make good decisions that will protect us, serve us and align with our highest purpose.

To get to where you want to go, you must first embrace where you are! There is no truly "bad" experiences. All experiences are simply learning, and growing opportunities handed to us to allow us the chance to apply the learnings. It is up to us whether we do or not. We only have ourselves to blame if we do not progress.

Nothing is happening to us. We are consciously creating all of the outcomes that come to life. This is the power of the mind itself and of the energies that surround it even more so. Taking the driver's seat back is imperative to getting where we want to go effectively and efficiently.

Would you trust the trajectory of your entire life and its purpose to an random driver??? That's a somewhat scary thought.

We must be proactive. There is no way to not be involved in our own lives. We reference things such as "getting tired" for our lack of drive to immerse fully in our internal and external landscape management. When honestly, we are the creators of this "inescapable" state we seek to escape from.

Stop and think about that for a second. If we created this state and designed it, inside and out, why do we convince ourselves it is so foreign or came from somewhere else that we cannot escape it? Silly right? That's right!

So, we begin by taking the wheel. We start by dusting off all the control room equipment left unattended. No matter how long something has been sitting, we can always bring it back to life through restoration. Think of this as just that, an instruction manual to restore the settings of your grand control facility to the state you choose for it to be now!

Just like a GPS, we all have a starting location regardless of where the ultimate destination we want to get to is. It simply allows us to gauge. It will reflect where we came from and all we have covered to get here at some point or another. Navigate. Congratulations on taking the wheel! Now let's get to work!

Everyone learns from someone else. It is how we have cultivated ourselves and evolved throughout time. There is never a reason to avoid coaching. Self-coaching. Peers. Mentors. Welcome. Knowledge. Always. We would not know our way without maps.

NOTES

THE UNLEARNING TECHNIQUE

That's right; you read that correctly. Or did you? Well, you didn't not, that's for sure! It likely means that there is no such thing, but let's think into it a little further to be sure.

Can you unlearn something? Why would you even want to in the first place? What purpose would that serve? When we look at things that we often get hung up on or perhaps skip past or do not see straight from a different angle, we can see so much more clearly that this is the meaning we were meant to see to begin with.

We cause all our greatest perception problems. Cause. Let's begin there. Think of things like a mathematic equation. To make sense of the problem, you must identify its components. Everything has a value. Everything a place. All the parts according to their roles equal an answer to the problem. Some strategy might need to be employed, perhaps conversion, etc. you can always work a problem forward and backward though. Perhaps it needs to be viewed from different perspectives to see the answer.

"IF YOU KEEP YOURSELF AT CENTER, YOU ARE ALWAYS PREPARED TO MOVE IN ANY DIRECTION" -ALAN WATTS

So, let's put this technique to good use. I want you to focus on something you learned that you don't feel you benefitted from in any way, shape, or form. It didn't make you see or realize anything at all. You think you didn't have anything to apply from this thing you learned that we would use this technique on. No gained understanding or perspective etc. We want a **complete** and total void for this technique to really work.

Alright, so you have it in mind then, right? You're ready to unlearn this learned aspect from which you never gained one thing.

At this point, you should all be realizing my humor. You may have tried to think with a little bit of delight that you did find something which met these contexts, although I know you inevitably only found error and humor. If we are being truthful, there is never, and yes, I used an absolute there to reference a time frame, a time where we did not learn something of value even from the best, worst, or most mundane of situations.

This technique is a bit of a "non technique." Who says it can't be effective in its application? We don't need as much substance, as we do the flip in perspective. Blowing a situation up and out of proportion helps us realize how silly we can be. We find we are the root of our own problems.

Once we realize this, it's amazing how much positive change can be affected. We can look at everything differently now. We will see the things we learn and unlearn *wink wink* differently now. So truly, perhaps this technique is a bit more effective than one would think. Perhaps then, in that aspect, "unlearning" some things are exactly what we need just to get a grip and regain perspective again.

It makes us grateful for the things we have learned and the details we did see. A place of gratitude is one of the most powerful states to be in when you desire to shift your mind, body, spirit, even reality itself. Our conscious mind plays tricks on us all the time. Often it would have us believe that we didn't gain as much as we have from the things we experience. We must learn the key is sorting through the noise of the conscious mind.

Tapping into the deep knowledge and understanding of the subconscious is the ultimate goal. Becoming more trusting and intuitive in our ancient instincts. Focus, connection, cerebralism everything we need is waiting on the other side of seeing the perspective. Things are not happening TO us. They are caused. Everything has a cause.

Like the math problems, things have roles, components, identities, etc. Life has cause. We must accept the responsibility of our place in the cause. It can offer us the greatest hope because if we are part of the cause of EVERYTHING well then, the future is bright! We can decide what way we want the EFFECTS to go. Through gained knowledge and understanding, we can DECIDE to do things differently. Different INPUT will always yield a different OUTPUT.

Anything else would be mathematically impossible *wink*

Much like "unlearning" things *wink wink*

What percentage (from 1-100) of things going on within your daily life do YOU believe yourself to be the cause of?

____

____

____

____

____

____

What would you decide differently if you knew you COULD not fail?

____

____

____

____

____

How would you put those things into play in the here & now?

____

____

____

____

____

What DO you want?

____

____

____

____

What do you see when you have what you want?

____

____

____

____

____

WHAT, which if you got it now, would remove your reasons for holding back from moving forward any longer now?

____

____

____

____

____

____

What feelings would IT bring to your life to have all of these positive changes now?

____

____

____

____

When you realize you have what it TAKES, it means you are capable of powerful change NOW.

____

____

____

____

NOTES

WHICH CAME FIRST C&E

We are not talking about chickens and eggs, nor wondering which one came first. We are wondering about the role of cause vs effect and how this vital concept shapes every part of our future.

Why do you want to take control, responsibility, and accountability?

As noble as they may be, your answers do not mean anything if you do not see from looking at things that you are the real reason you are not where you want to be or have the things you want to have.

It does not matter if you seek material things or intangibles like peace, freedom, balance, etc. What matters is that you fully and undeniably understand your role in it all. The truth is it is all because of you. Let's take part of that word out and sit with CAUSE for a moment. I'll explain.

Often, we go through life thinking things are happening TO us, not DUE TO us. Big difference. Technically, are we not consciously creating our ENTIRE experience here in this life? Do we really get into "accidents"? Do things just miraculously and "randomly" happen to us by happenstance? Or do we invite and evoke things?

It's a brain bender for sure, but is that not the point that while we are here, we are learning, exploring and growing accordingly?! If this is the case, then the commonality is that we must question even what we think we know. If we have purposes and paths in destiny, then what we are subconsciously choosing will weigh heavily in what comes to be in the here & now.

If you have ever had a massage, you know how good it can make your body feel afterward- bringing with it numerous health benefits. Same for a great workout, right?! It makes you feel you accomplished something that will better you later. Make you look good outside, feel good inside. So then, why do we not massage our minds with different perspectives and learning? Why do we not spend time working our minds out like we do our bodies?

We place so much importance on the health of everything else we sometimes slip past what drives it all to begin with. Even then, our spirit and consciousness surpass it all. To bring it back to the realm of the living - even after death, the heart continues to beat some, but the brain will remain active even longer. We cannot even explain all why oddities like this exist.

If the mind has such control over the physical and the metaphysical, why don't we prioritize it more? That is a simple answer; you don't have to google the definition of any words to figure out no one ever taught us.

It is not manageable or profitable when people are empowered over their own health. To know, they could create all their own successes.

How at CAUSE are you?

0 - None

I think I am a victim of all circumstances and have zero control over things. Therefore, life takes me in any direction it wants to, or so I believe.

1- Very very little

I listen to external sources but struggle with any decision, so I feel stuck and helpless most of the time. I am drained from constant conflict internally.

2-Very little

I will listen to outside influences, which will usually dictate my choices. I'm not always happy with those choices.

3- Some

I constantly oscillate in an irregular pattern of decision-making, drive, and thought process— some of my own, some of the environment around me.

4- Somewhat stable

I feel as though I make sound decisions and see those results at times, although the reasons or consistency seem to allude me.

5- Mild progress

I feel half of the time I am in tune and creating a good future for myself, yet the other half seems to be still ping-ponging around.

6- Past mid point

I realize I am creating my life. I'm conscious of the process, yet know I still have learning to do. There is room to grow and improve to get to where I truly want to be.

7- Heading up

I'm getting better day by day. I am open to accepting new knowledge and power; only occasionally do I not remember I am the reason everything is happening how it is.

8- Steep climb

I am often uncomfortable in realizing hard truths about how I am doing, what I am thinking, saying, etc. and how things manifest into life.

9- Near peak

I feel I am accepting full responsibility almost all the time. I feel happy, sound of mind, body & spirit and in balance with the universe.

10- Enlightenment

I see now I am everything— all the time. There is no beginning and no end, and I am everything in between. I am all creation. I am pure energy. Pure love.

NOTES

YEAR IN REVIEW

———————

Let's take some time to review the last year of your life and the decisions you've made. Pencil in the significant changes in each area, then let's rank how we felt we did in those areas use a 0-5 scale 0 being void of action or did not get any desired results up to 5, which means success and happiness in your endeavors.

Career-

Health & Wellbeing-

Family-

Friends-

Personal growth & self development-

Romance/Relationships-

Fun & play-

Finances-

Let's also take some time to investigate your personal habits and see where we have room to develop and can work to grow.

Sleep-

Sex-

Activity-

Exercise-

Relaxation-

Stress management-

Strength-

Nutrition-

Spirituality-

Immunity-

Consistency-

Joy & happiness-

What area of your life do you believe needs your attention most now?

____

____

____

____

____

How can you be more present in the here & now to affect the most significant change in these things?

____

____

____

____

____

Within what timeline are you expecting to see change from yourself?

____

____

____

____

____

What do you already know you will be grateful for from this process?

____

____

____

____

When you have what you want, what do you see, hear, feel and where are you?

____

____

____

____

____

As we work from examining, realizing, becoming more aware, to learning - now to doing, then into setting future outcomes, we will show you how flexibility is the framework. Flexibility allows this house you are building on its solid foundation to breathe and flex no matter the element that it faces.

"Those who allow themselves flexibility in every circumstance are most likely to rule the system"

- Law of requisite variety

NOTES

RELEASE IS LEARNED

Have you ever had to let go? Did it feel painful? Was it a difficult process? Did it almost feel like losing something you identified as a part of yourself?

This is normal and natural. We place heavy attachments onto things for many emotional reasons. Learning to be able and capable of healthy release is something less often taught than even practiced.

This process is something we should hand down to our children. Just think, do you remember the struggle of the first time you were forced to let go? Do you wish you had a safe environment and trusted partner to help teach you to release before being forced out into the reality of it in the world?

Honestly, if you have children of any age, I urge you to revisit this concept with them. Yes, math, history, science are all-important but equally so are how to effectively deal with loss, hurt, rejection, disappointment, emotions of all kinds. Letting go is a delicate art of itself. When to let go and how to let go with kindness and grace. It is knowing how to navigate and communicate those boundaries - when to identify whether something is good for us or not.

These skills and more that we will touch on here are vital to saving us from unnecessary hurt. Preventing us also time wasted that can be focused more successfully onto the endeavors we invest ourselves into. A simple teaching opportunity can free up an entire portion within a lifetime.

(The origin of the word release itself is 'deliverance')

"PRACTICE GIVING THINGS AWAY, NOT JUST THINGS YOU DO NOT CARE ABOUT EITHER, ALSO THINGS YOU DO LIKE.

REMEMBER, IT IS NOT THE SIZE OF A GIFT YET ITS QUALITY AND THE AMOUNT OF MENTAL ATTACHMENT YOU OVERCOME IN ORDER TO GIVE IT AWAY.

GIVE THOUGHT TO GIVING.
GIVE THINGS CAREFULLY.
OBSERVE THE MENTAL PROCESS THAT GOES ALONG WITH THE ACT OF RELEASING THAT LITTLE THING YOU LIKED."

-HUSTON SMITH,
TIBETAN BOOK OF THE DEAD

TAKE 10 STONES

You will need 10 large rough river rocks for this exercise

As well as non toxic waterproof paint and small brushes

These things are easily and inexpensively found at a craft or other store or even perhaps gathered naturally in part too

Once acquired you will have one hour to sit and paint these stones in any way you please

Take this time to enjoy the process of creating

Revel in time to play and paint without a defined purpose

Simply be

Find the joy in expression

Once stones are painted allow them time to dry

Take fully dried stones and go to any nearby or available body of water where allowable or to an area of wilderness in nature

Proceed to toss or leave all of your stones

Taking as little time as you need to experience the process of letting something you spent time on go

Spend time appreciating the time you put into creating

Knowing that in giving away these stones now you gain

You grow

You have learned to let go now!

NOTES

REAL REFLECTION

Even if you are social, extroverted, and outgoing, you must become comfortable spending grounding time alone in your presence. This builds and develops your character and soul. It increases your strength and stamina.

This will also help you safely confront and make peace with things you avoid now. Sit comfortably in front of a mirror. Set a timer for 5 minutes. Make constant eye contact. Remain silent and simply breathe. Just notice all that you need to.

What thoughts come and go?

____

____

____

____

____

____

____

____

What do you notice about your physical appearance?

____

____

____

____

____

What emotions come forward?

____

____

____

____

____

What important things is your body trying to tell you?

____

____

____

____

____

What is it asking you for more of?

____

____

____

____

____

What are you grateful for?

____

____

____

____

____

What are you proud of yourself for?

____

____

____

____

____

What do you feel you are doing right?

____

____

____

____

____

What are you learning right now?

____

____

____

____

____

What do you want?

____

____

____

____

____

What can you let go of that no longer serves you?

____

____

____

____

____

What will you allow yourself to unearth that has been buried?

____

____

____

____

____

What are you afraid of?

____

____

____

____

____

What purpose does it all serve?

____

____

____

____

____

____

What is your highest intention?

____

____

____

____

____

What is your responsibility to others?

____

____

____

____

____

____

What is your responsibility to yourself?

____

____

____

____

____

____

____

What are any closing thoughts or feelings you have?

____

____

____

____

____

____

____

____

"WE ARE ALL JARS OF CLAY, FRAGILE, POOR, YET WE CARRY WITHIN US AN IMMENSE TREASURE."

-POPE FRANCIS

WHO ARE YOU?

———————————

I am...

I am...

I am...

I am...

I am...

I am...

I am...

I am...

I am...

I am...

(Changing who you are is as easy as changing your "I am")

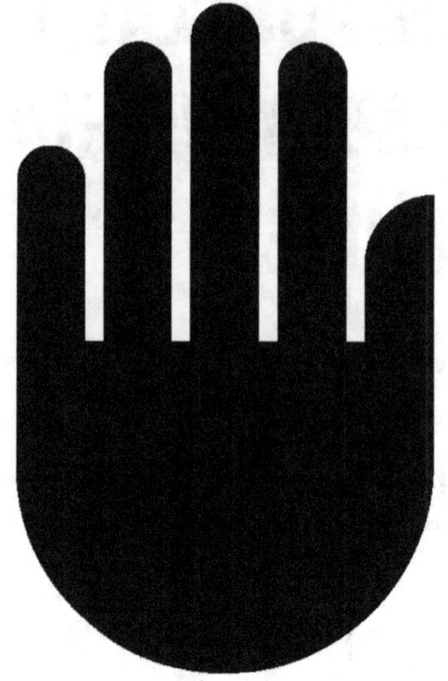

This is LIFE or DEATH, so please imagine that as you tell...

What are the 5 most essential things in your life?

If there was a gun to your head, what could you not live without? What are your non-negotiables, your deal breakers?

1.

2.

3.

4.

5.

Does this align with who you want to be? Are changes needed?

"AND ABOVE ALL, WATCH WITH GLITTERING EYES THE WHOLE WORLD AROUND YOU BECAUSE THE GREATEST SECRETS ARE ALWAYS HIDDEN IN THE MOST UNLIKELY PLACES. THOSE WHO DO NOT BELIEVE IN MAGIC WILL NEVER FIND IT."

-ROALD DAHL

NOTES

WHAT DO YOU BELIEVE IN?

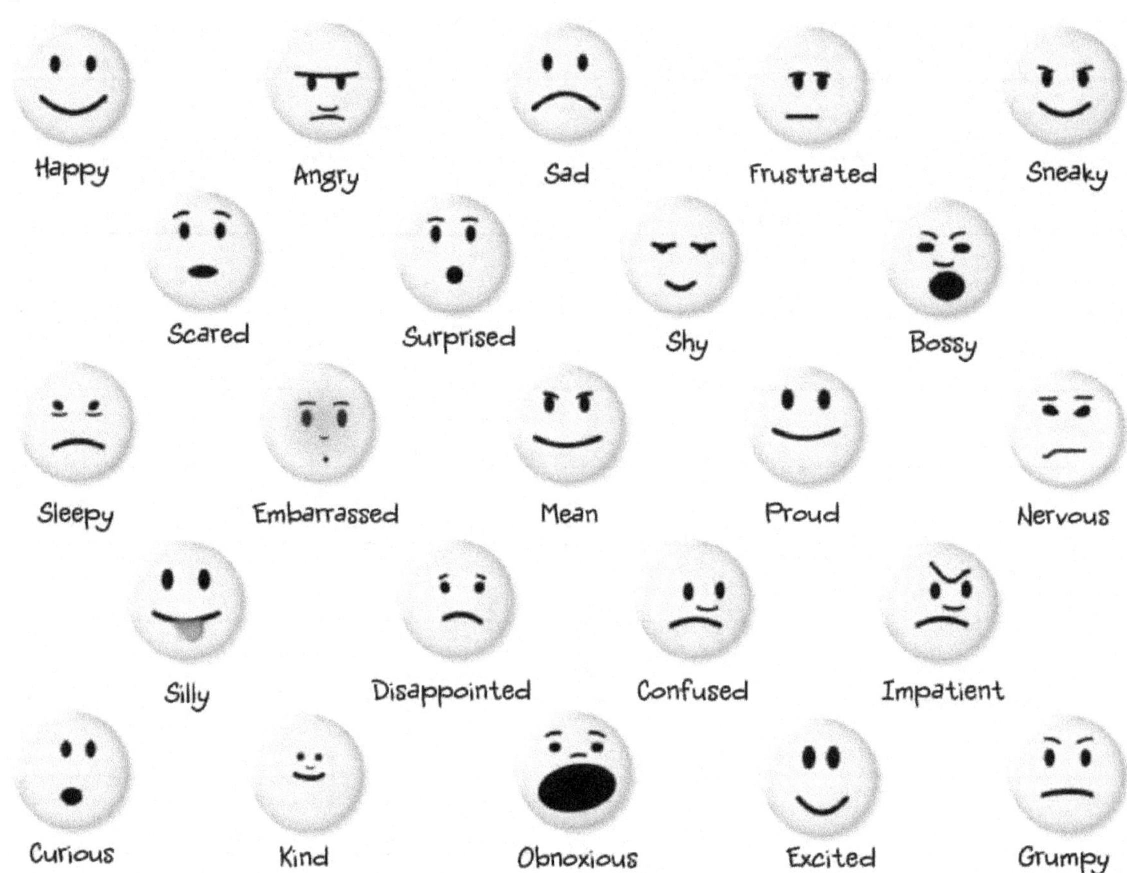

Check Yo-self Before You Wreck Yo-self

How are you behaving based on how you feel?

How are the things you see, hear, and feel
in your environment affecting this?

What are some things you can do NOW to adjust
any unwarranted reactions?

You do not need to stop any emotion or behavior;
you simply must manage them.

NOTES

BLAST THAT!

When did you decide that? Based on what? According to whom? These are my greatest gifts to empower you to blast out negative emotions and limiting decisions about yourself.

At a point in the past, events made you create an adverse decision that still affects you, although it no longer serves your purpose or even applies to who you are now! Here's how to blast that!

Negative Beliefs:

"I don't believe I deserve...

"I don't believe I can...

WHEN DID YOU DECIDE THAT?

Doubts:

"I wouldn't be able to....

"I can't do...

"I'd lose...

"I'm not good enough to...

"I'm afraid I would...

"I may not do well...

"I will fail...

WHEN DID YOU DECIDE THAT?

____

____

____

____

____

____

____

____

____

____

____

____

Comparisons:

"All I want is a *better* life....

"Wish I could make *more* money...

WHEN DID YOU DECIDE THAT?

____

____

____

____

____

____

____

____

____

____

____

____

____

Indirect Feeling:
"I'm just not happy....
"I don't feel loved...

WHEN DID YOU DECIDE THAT?

____

____

____

____

____

____

____

____

____

____

____

____

____

SMART PEOPLE SWEAR

____

Negations:

"I don't...

"I won't...

"I can't...

"I shouldn't...

"I wouldn't...

"I couldn't...

"I'm not...

WHEN DID YOU DECIDE THAT?

____

____

____

____

____

____

____

____

____

____

____

____

Psy-Issues:

"I can't focus...

"I can't sit still long enough to...

"I can't quiet my mind...

"I can't sleep...

WHEN DID YOU DECIDE THAT?

____

____

____

____

____

____

____

____

____

____

____

____

____

Accidents:

"I was late to work because...

"I missed an event due to...

"I couldn't get approved...

"I fell off track...

WHEN DID YOU DECIDE THAT?

____

____

____

____

____

____

____

____

____

____

____

____

____

Negative Emotion:

"Fear holds me back…

"I get angry and it makes me…

"My sadness…

"The grief was just…

"I was too embarrassed to…

"I'm just not confident about…

WHEN DID YOU DECIDE THAT?

____

____

____

____

____

____

____

____

____

____

____

____

____

"IF YOU DO NOT HAVE A PROBLEM. DO YOU REALLY NEED A SOLUTION?"

- ME

NOTES

LET'S GET FLIPPY WITH IT

You get stuck sometimes. We all do. Here is an easy & effortless way to break up the problem.

Simply run through the series of questions-

1. What's wrong?

2. What caused this problem?

3. How have you failed to resolve this?

4. How can you overcome the solution to your problem?

5. What would you like to change?

6. When will you STOP IT from being a limitation?

7. How many ways do you know you have solved this?

8. How do you now know you are changing and seeing things differently now

Thought provoking questions are one of the greatest aids for learning and growing. Use these all at once or try one daily to keep yourself developing this healthy mindset

Why do you love yourself?

____

____

____

____

____

What mistake have you yet to forgive yourself for and why?

____

____

____

____

____

What is a time in life that you settled for less than what you deserved, and how did you learn from it?

____

____

____

____

____

If you were ever lost, where would you go to find yourself?

____

____

____

____

____

Who is responsible for your happiness?

____

____

____

____

____

How are they handling that responsibility?

____

____

____

____

____

What do you miss most about yourself?

____

____

____

____

____

If your attention was an arrow, what have you been aiming at lately?

____

____

____

____

____

In what ways are you guarding your heart? Are those healthy ways?

____

____

____

____

____

____

What lines do you draw with people that they should not cross? What happens if they do?

____

____

____

____

____

If saying "No" was a form of self-love, what is a time you wish you would have loved yourself more by doing so?

____

____

____

____

____

When you are most happy, how can you live in more of those moments from now on?

____

____

____

____

____

Describe a time in the past where you spoke negativity into existence and how that influenced failure?

____

____

____

____

____

As a child, is this how you imagined your life would be?

____

____

____

____

____

Is what you accept from others what you think you deserve?

____

____

____

____

____

____

Which parts of yourself do you give others, before they have earned them, and how can you set boundaries to protect that process?

____

____

____

____

____

____

What's hard to do, yet you're going to do anyway to reach your goals?

____

____

____

____

____

In what ways can you step outside your comfort zone to take hold of the things you want most?

____

____

____

____

____

In what ways has forgiving the person who hurt you helped you grow?

____

____

____

____

____

What has your most significant mistake cost you, and what did you learn from that?

____

____

____

____

What principles will you stand on to keep you grounded if things around you ever fall?

____

____

____

____

What are you most passionate about in life, and how is that bearing fruit in your life right now?

____

____

____

____

____

Is it possible to love yourself more, and if so, why aren't you?

____

____

____

____

What are some standards you hold yourself and others to in your relationships?

____

____

____

____

____

What five qualities must someone possess to become close to you? Does this need adjustment?

____

____

____

____

____

In what ways have you grown from your last failure?

____

____

____

____

____

What type of person does the person you dream about, dream about?

____

____

____

____

____

When was the last time you allowed negativity to snatch a piece of your peace? How can you prevent that from happening again?

____

____

____

____

____

What do you do that you don't thank yourself for enough?

____

____

____

____

Are you giving your all to yourself? If not, why?

____

____

____

____

____

What environment do you thrive most in? Are you currently in this environment? Why or why not?

____

____

____

____

____

Are you fully healed from your previous relationships? If not, what still hurts?

____

____

____

____

If you married yourself today, what would your vows of commitment to yourself be?

____

____

____

____

____

What are you lying to yourself about, and why are you afraid of the truth?

____

____

____

____

____

____

Which parts of your life do you need to be more careful in choosing who you give access to?

____

____

____

____

What actions do you take to support your love for yourself?

____

____

____

____

What are your soul's deepest desires?

____

____

____

____

____

____

What can you do to move your body more to show it support?

____

____

____

____

____

When do you take moments of mindful pause to reflect on all your progress?

____

____

____

____

____

____

If everything you hear or see feeds your mind, what type of mental diet have you been on?

____

____

____

____

____

____

____

____

____

____

____

____

____

____

A CHILD'S INNOCENCE

Write a letter to yourself as a child. Explain everything in great detail. Where would you invite them to play more? What would you tell them about you now?

What reconciliations could you make?

____

____

____

____

____

Was there a dream to follow that you let go of for more "practical" reasons that perhaps should be remembered?

____

____

____

____

____

What pitfalls might you warn them to avoid, and how specifically? What should they enjoy more of before they grow up?

____

____

____

____

____

____

____

____

Like a big brother or sister looking out for their best interest, what guidance could you offer them to hold them over for the rest of their lifetime?

____

____

____

____

____

____

____

What can prepare them for heartache? What do they see once they pass it?

____

____

____

____

____

____

____

What can they do to become a better and more successful adult someday?

____

____

____

____

____

____

____

____

NOTES

TAKE ME TO CHURCH

I personally am not per se religious; one might say my religion is Love itself. Let's stage an event, though because its purpose holds great power in transformation.

Please write your eulogy. That's right. If you were deceased and had to stand up like your family and friends who will one day and speak about yourself because you had passed on... What would you have to say about yourself?

That's about as stark and sobering as it gets, and no, you can not avoid this; it is paramount to your success in creating significant change in your life now!

So, grab the tissues and get to work!

What would you say at your funeral in front of the people who love you?

Take ample time to reflect on this exercise and perhaps even revisit it often.

____

____

____

____

____

Do I achieve my own goals? Why or why not?

____

____

____

____

What services do I provide myself and others? Are those the kind of quality I, myself, would even appreciate?

____

____

____

____

____

When I give, do I give QUALITY or QUANTITY? What can I adjust if I am unhappy with this?

____

____

____

____

____

Why do I procrastinate, and how can I be more driven?

____

____

____

____

Do I like my personality, and if not, what changes can I make to be satisfied?

____

____

____

____

____

Would I date me?

____

____

____

____

____

Would I want to work with me?

____

____

____

____

____

Would I want to be married to me?

____

____

____

____

____

____

____

Am I the embodiment of my ideal mate already?

Do I make decisions quickly, confidently, and efficiently?

Do I have regrets, and if so, why? What needs need to be met in order to feel confident?

How is my follow-up? How is my follow through?

____

____

____

____

____

Am I over cautious?

____

____

____

____

____

Am I under cautious?

____

____

____

____

____

____

Am I open-minded?

____

____

____

____

____

Do I realize everyone is just doing the best they can with what they have where they are, including me?

____

____

____

____

____

Do I respect all people's versions of the world even when I disagree with it?

____

____

____

____

____

Am I open-minded?

Do I have internal or external conflicts to resolve?

____

____

____

____

____

____

Do I budget my time, energy, expenses, and is this benefitting me?

____

____

____

____

____

____

Am I unfair to anyone, including myself? If so, in what ways can I rectify this for the future?

____

____

____

____

____

Am I in the correct career field?

____

____

____

____

____

____

____

What would make you happier today, and why are you not following it more?

____

____

____

____

____

____

____

____

NOTES

WHY AFFIRMATIONS DON'T WORK

Your subconscious mind knows what ideas are its own and which are not. Do not use cookie-cutter generic affirmations to obtain the success you seek in life!

When using affirmations, make sure they are your own and make them SPECIFIC, like manifestations. How will you get what you desire if you are not asking for the exact and right things?

Today I am...

My body is...

I am superior to...

I have been given...

I forgive those who...

A river of compassion washes...

I am guided in my every step to...

I possess the qualities to...

My business is...

Creative energy is...

Happiness is...

My ability to....

I deserve to...

My thoughts are filled with...

Today, I abandon...

Many people...

I am blessed with...

Everything is happening now because...
I acknowledge my self worth because...
People look up to me because...
I have...
I want...
I need...
I am a powerhouse for...
Though these times are rough...
This phase of my life...
My future...
My past does not...
My ideal projection is...
The perfect partner for me is...
I see...
I hear...
I feel...
I think...
I radiate...
I believe...
This conquering of...
The trajectory for...
My future is...
My efforts are...
My dreams...
My fears of tomorrow are simply...
I am at peace with...
My nature is...
My life is just...
I woke up today...
I lay my head down tonight and...
With every breath I...

Creation is within me, and I choose…
If I could know no failure I…
I can…
I will…
I am…
My life is…
It's profound that…
Life provides…

NOTES

THE LABYRINTH OF LIFE

Walking a labyrinth, which is a type of maze, even with your fingertips, becomes the most beautiful meditative process. If you struggle to focus and this holds you back from traditional meditation, may this help you.

Like a labyrinth, there is one way in and one way out. The path may wind around, yet the final destination is sure. At the center, there is always clarity. This approach can bring us deep peace; perhaps we have never known.

Labyrinths come from the Middle Ages and are used to focus the mind. Beautiful geometrical patterns for walking or tracing keep thought moving in a direction with less wandering. Used as a tool for higher consciousness and embraced in traditions worldwide.

Allowing your mind to unwind can sometimes be a challenge. Now you can learn a fun way of unraveling without falling apart. Feel how freeing it is to come to relaxation. Visually remain engaged as you go. Use your time to think along with the labyrinth.

There are only positives that this brings for you. Think of your life as you enter. Bring your thoughts forward so you may understand them as you progress the labyrinth's path. There exists no right or wrong; know you are in a place of neutrality.

What will you gain in thought and, through reflection, welcome it to you when entering?

As you come to center, what do you have to be thankful for already?

As you reverse, what can you apply from this into your life now, the doing of which will benefit you?

As you leave, what can you release that you no longer need to hold on to?

As you exit, what do you wish to see for yourself or others in your future?

Just like life, we sometimes forget, it is not a maze meant to trap us. It has defined ways but requires conscious thought to get through. When you show up for it, it shows up for you.

ENJOY THE JOURNEY

THE SECRET IS, THERE IS NO SECRET, YOU JUST HAVE TO PUT ONE FOOT IN FRONT OF THE OTHER!

Action is the cure for fear.

If you are only ever motivated by pain, what happens when you run out of it?

Think about the five people you spend the most time with. Do you really want to be like these people?

Nothing can be done without Hope and Confidence.

Persistence is a great substitute for talent.

If you want to do it, write it down!

You don't become what you want; you become what you believe.

Dare to fail.

Gratitude turns everything into enough.

Decide what kind of life you want, then say NO to everything else.

Energy flows where intention goes.

Every "NO" brings you closer to "YES"

NOTES

HO'OPONOPONO

Dr. Ihaleakala Hew Len- cured an entire ward of criminally insane patients without ever meeting any of them or spending a single moment in the same room as them.

You heal others by first healing yourself. This is another of many reasons why you must be your own greatest priority before others— self-identity through Ho'oponopono.

There is no "out there." We experience everything in our minds. There is only "in here." Truly everything you see, hear, every person you meet, you experience inside your mind. There's no backyard, only what's inside the house of your mind, so do you see what you have such control over already.

You can clean your mental house.

Organize. Redecorate. Restore. Renovate.

The order in which you perform the principles of this practice is not important, only that you do complete all of them.

Forgiveness.

Repentance.

Gratitude.

Love.

When you hold resentment toward another, you are bound to that person or condition by an emotional link that is stronger than steel. Forgiveness is the only way to dissolve that link and get free.

Ho'oponopono means to "make right" and is the Hawaiian word for forgiveness. Opono-pono is repetitive because doing it twice gives energy to the bond breaking or bond building.

Through your light body, you are connected with all of life. Through your emotion, you always affect everyone around you by your thoughts, words, feelings, and actions.

The full moon is a wonderful and blessed time to perform Ho'oponopono as the natural electro-magnetic forces of the waning moon act to assist you in the process of letting go.

Through performing the Ho'oponopono forgiveness meditation, you will be loving and accepting the shadow, lost parts of yourself, and powerfully activating the law of grace to operate fully in your life.

Through the power of grace, you can know the blessing of absolute and unconditional self-love and acceptance.

In truth, when you love yourself completely, you love everything and everyone through all dimensions of time and space.

This simple act of transmutation (the taking in of one energy, cleansing it, and transforming it or putting it back out as a better source), bringing your darkness into the light, provides incredible nourishment and frees your soul.

Ho'oponopono forgiveness meditation empowers you to shine with brilliance and renewed self-love and respect.

Ho'oponopono in essence, means to make things right with your ancestors or make right with the people with whom you are connected and have relationships.

And, most significantly, it reconnects, deepens, and heals your relationship with yourself.

Your self-trust will rise exponentially as you perform a regular practice of letting go of any grievances against others or self-blame!

In Eastern cultures, there is a tradition of honoring your ancestors.

Being aligned with and cleansing ancestral relations is considered essential for harmonic prosperity at all levels.

Without reverence and gratitude for one's ancestors, prosperous circumstances will always be severely limited.

In Japan, China, and the Hawaiian tradition, it's crucial to cleanse any past problems you may have had in relationships, especially with one's relatives.

There may also be family patterns you do not want to continue.

Generational themes are often passed along through the family lineage, like depression, poverty consciousness, addiction, or other unfortunate character traits.

Ho'oponopono allows you to cleanse your ancestral lineage.

This cleansing and healing of relationships within your family lineage brings you the highest and greatest good fortune!

Calm your mind and sit quietly. Allow yourself to be quietly present with yourself.

Light your white candle and focus on the flame. The candle's light reflects the divine spark of light within you.

Remember that what you see in another is a reflection, something within you, so all healing is self-healing. And all forgiveness is self-forgiveness.

Focus Ho'oponopono on every person in your life with whom you feel misaligned.

You may repeat the Ho'oponopono meditation as needed to cleanse all negative emotional blockages within yourself and between yourself and others (people, organizations, places, or situations).

SET YOUR INTENTION

Step 1 - See the person (organization, place, situation, or an aspect of yourself) with whom you feel discomfort within a healing circle of light.

Step 2 - See yourself within this same healing circle of light.

Step 3 - See a beautiful golden cord of light above your head connecting you with your greater self

Step 4 - See a golden cord above the other person's head to their greater self

Step 5 - Then, see a golden cord of light between your greater self and the other person's greater self.

Step 6 - Now, see a golden cord of light from your heart to the other person's heart. Feel the free flow of love moving through the golden cord of light connecting you with the other person.

You've created a protective energy grid of light to ground the healing energy of Ho'oponopono forgiveness meditation and amplify its effect.

Your greater selves stand as witnesses to your sincere intention to release the past and light the process for the highest good of all.

ACTIVATE HO'OPONOPONO

Now activate Ho'oponopono with your intention to heal any split or feeling of separation between you and another.

First by saying with genuine feeling, "I apologize," and then, "Please forgive me."

You say this to focus your awareness on the thought or feeling that has gotten into your mind-body system, like a virus, disrupting your peace of mind and heart-based love energies.

You don't need to know why or understand why you feel the way you do.

*If necessary, and you desire to completely sever all ties to this person, place, feeling, thing, situation, etc., simply envision a pair of scissors in your hand and cut the golden light cord.

Thus, freeing yourself and the thing of each other's energy.

By saying, "I apologize," you are asking for forgiveness inside yourself in order to release and let go of the feeling of discomfort inside of you.

Forgiveness does not mean you are condoning anyone's behavior. Forgiveness simply means you no longer wish to suffer from a past issue.

End by saying, "I love you," followed by, "Thank you."

Continue repeating, "I love you" and "Thank you," for as long as needed until you feel completely free.

You may return to perform Ho'oponopono again if needed until you feel complete resolution at the core of your being.

Remember to breathe deeply and exhale as you let go of any toxic emotions and stagnant energy.

The sound of the words, "I love you," acts to transmute the vibration of energy from stuck to flowing now.

"I love you" reconnects you to your wholeness.

Conclude your Ho'oponopono meditation with "Thank you" to express your gratitude that harmony has been restored.

NOTES

MIND ~ BODY

K eeping your brain and body healthy is essential. You can also obtain excellent health by building your consciousness up.

Daily walking is not only a great activity for the body; it allows a few moments of space for you to do mindful reflection as well.

Begin and end each day by saying three things you are grateful for out loud.

Read an inspirational quote each day.

Getting 15 minutes of sunlight between 8:30 am - 10:30 am is proven to increase serotonin levels, the happiness hormone within our bodies.

Getting 15 minutes of sunlight in the evening between 4:30 pm - 5:30 pm showed increases in melatonin, the hormone that helps us sleep more restfully.

Drinking your body weight in ounces of water will help most bodily functions, and when the body is happy, the mind is happy.

Start and end every day while sitting or lying in bed by taking ten deep belly breaths and pausing to hold each for a moment. When exhaling, literally slowly push all the air out— squeezing your belly gradually harder as you release all the air.

BUZZ WORD ALERT!

As they say, trends are your friends, so let's talk about manifestation. It is seen more currently as a popular way to get what you want.

Yes! You can bring about quite literally all the success and future outcomes you choose to by simply focusing your mind intently. There are a few tricks to this process, though.

Don't be vague! State your desire very, very, and I mean VERY specifically. If you simply say you want a sweater for your birthday, do not be surprised when you get grandma's fuzzy pink flamingo sweater instead of cashmere.

Be SPECIFIC!!! If you want to make money... be SPECIFIC... A million dollars is roughly 5-6 hundred thousand after taxes. So, do you want 500 thousand or a mil? Pay attention.

If you're looking for love, better specify what qualities and traits that person will have, better make sure they are even available in the first place, lol! SPECIFY THE DETAILS

You can never have too many details.

This way, you will know FOR SURE when your manifestations arrive into your life because it will feel and seem as though they have already been there. A Deja vu of sorts because you have already fully imagined them time and time again within your mind and daily practices.

To bring these manifestations to life, it helps to write them down on a piece of paper and either keep it where you can see it often or tuck it under your pillow at night.

Don't tuck it in a wallet, for example, because it's out of sight, out of mind, and quickly forgotten. The universe intuitively knows you must not want it badly enough if it is easily forgotten.

Likewise, write down your manifestations and tape them to any glass bottle of water after removing labels or making sure what you have written can be seen. (not blocked by anything) Adhere your statements facing inward toward the water.

Speak your wishes in detail, exactly, out loud to your water before you take a drink and as often as is felt needed.

Also, know when it comes to manifestation, you cannot simply ask the universe for all these nice things you desire and then sit there on your ass with your hands out, just expecting it to fall into your lap.

Get off your ass and do the work to bring it to life. This may also mean working on yourself to ensure you are ready for your manifestation. For example, with love: Are you your ideal partner's partner? If not, you'd better get your ass to work!

Visualize every detail frequently. Vividly. Imagine how every detail comes to life inside your mind and tickles all your senses. What do you hear? How does it look? Can you smell, even taste it? Does it bring on strong emotion? See yourself accepting it. Welcome it and embrace it fully and completely throughout time and into the future.

You must release to receive. For the old to clear out we must make space for the new. Begin decluttering in whatever ways are needed to make room physically and energetically for the arrival of your manifestation.

Let your behavior lead. If you are asking for loyalty, dedication, commitment, etc., then be prepared to ante up! Better throw out all those old photos with exes. Quit flirting with other people in meaningless banter while wasting time on social media late at night out of boredom or desperation. Keep your word to yourself when you say you'll do things.

Start embodying what you see as the ideal mirror reflection to your manifestation. Guess it's a great time to work on being more selfless instead of selfish.

There's a lot more work to be done on manifesting than many think. It's more than just running around screaming things into the sky, as if you will just be granted all of them, like unlimited wishes from a genie in a bottle. I mean, magic exists; it's just more... practical than that.

Practical Magic, perhaps.

NOTES

ARE YOU BOARD?

One great way to bring your wishes, dreams, and manifestations to life is to create a vision board.

A vision board can be a poster board full of cut outs, a simple collage of cropped photos on your phone, use an app, draw, paint; the sky is the limit! You have creative freedom here. All you must do is visually remind yourself of what you want.

This is also a great practice to help get you back to being innocent and taking time for play and self-exploration. We get far too far into our routines at times and sometimes need the refreshment of getting off the beaten path.

Create freely and without expectation. Expectations will only result in future resentments. What purpose would that serve? That's right! NONE.

We want what we want, and we want it now! It's only natural. So having creative activities that co-align with your highest purposes, principles, and manifestations will bring the most remarkable result with ease and minimal effort.

You will learn, as well as become practiced in patience. In the process of gaining a benefit, all of us can never not acquire more skills.

Keep your vision board visible and updated often.

FUTURE OUTCOMES

It's time to make the final map of your goals. Now that you have accomplished a tremendous amount of exploration within yourself, your mind, body, and soul, you are ready to emerge anew!

We are taking all the learnings and applying them here. We will draft a map of the landscape of your goals, both internal as well as external.

Becoming PRESENT and dictating these goals this way.

When will you have it? SPECIFICALLY

____

____

____

____

____

What will it be?

____

____

____

____

____

How will you know you have it?

____

____

____

____

____

Where do you see yourself once you have it?

____

____

____

____

____

Paint yourself that picture fully and completely, imagine it

____

____

____

____

____

____

What do you hear all around you there in that destination?

____

____

____

____

____

Who is with you?

____

____

____

____

What are the deep, intense feelings overwhelming you?

____

____

____

____

____

____

What sensations do you experience?

____

____

____

____

____

____

____

How does it affect the rest of your life?

____

____

____

____

____

____

____

WHO'S YOUR SUPERHERO

Our time together has come to an end. Please enjoy locking in your progress and success with this guided hypnosis as a parting gift.

Loosen and relax your eyes as easily as you can now; if this is being read or recited to you, you may close your eyes now instead of trying to fight it. It's just too hard. Thats right, just relaxing further now.

Imagine all of those things you don't like about yourself- insecurities, fears, negative desires and temptations, past regrets, limiting beliefs...

All of it.

Imagine it all as it takes on another entity. Someone who looks like you but embodies all of those negative things you don't like standing up from your chair and walking across the room as they turn around and look back at you.

Realizing that all those qualities were there for a purpose- they served you through certain situations, helped you cope, at times even helping you learn- 'Thank them for serving you as best they could in those situations.'

Tell that old you that 'you love them.' Feel the love inside your body for the old you because you've grown beyond it. Hear that old you say back, 'I love you too.'

Tell the old you that 'I accept you and I forgive you unconditionally,' realizing that anything that was done or said was what they thought was the best choice at the time, and now you've grown.

Say, 'I forgive you' and feel the unconditional forgiveness as they say back, 'I accept you, and I forgive you unconditionally too.'

I want you to imagine now that the shell around that body becomes transparent, and inside you can see a dark, dank, dirty fluid filling the shell. Tell the old you 'I release you.'

Notice as valves in the fingers and toes open, and that old, dirty fluid drains out of the fingers and toes, out into the ground where it can return back to positive source energy.

Imagine a bright orange industrial strength cleaning light as it beams down from the skyward, down through the crown of their head, filling the body from the toes up. This light fills the body like a fluid and scrubs, rinses, and cleans the entire inside of that body, removing all impurities.

As the valves open in the fingers and toes, allowing all the orange fluid to drain out into the ground, again where it can return back to positive source energy.

Ask 'Now, who is your favorite superhero? Who is your hero, mentor, or idol? Who is that person whose qualities you want for yourself?'

Good. Imagine that new body takes on the physiology of that person. All those traits are beginning to shine through. Imagine a bright white light coming down from the skyward- the loving light of the universe.

Filling that body with all those qualities of that hero and any other qualities you want for yourself. Watch as it tops off and the outer shell resembles the new you.

Now stand in the new body.

Feel as it integrates into you and you into it, at the cellular level, becoming one.

Now bring your eyes back to the present and open them fully. Enjoying the experience, you just had take a deep heavy breath and exhaled. Upon exhaling, notice how everything is just different NOW.

Did you know? It does not matter where you are coming from. All that matters is where you are going.

We are all made up of the same things you find in nature all around you. Just as nature renews itself, so can you.

The power of choice is such a powerful tool.

If you can take anything away from this, let it be this:

You do not need a past in order to have a future.

I know you're changing and seeing things differently now. Realize you'll have success in future outcomes thanks, in part, and whole because of these insights you have adopted now into yourself as your own!

Go and be awesome!

Who can you help today, who perhaps once was just like you?

Thank You for *click* locking in your mindset with me!

ABOUT THE AUTHOR

Amy Vandagriff comes from a small town but has a vision of the big picture. With a background in business, linguistics and a lifetime of experience navigating challenges, obstacles, and opportunities, she discovered that her methods should be shared. Amy's formal education coupled with her enlightenment gave her a strong purpose to help others, just as others once helped herself, to pay it forward. Amy's goal is to make alternative practices for mindset and mental health more readily available for those who desire to change their lives and create a life they desire.

Master Practitioner of Neurolinguistic Programming MPNLP

Master Practitioner of Hypnosis MPHt

Master Practitioner of Life & Success Coaching MPLC

Our way of giving back is to work with foundations for the support of suicide prevention, mental health awareness, learning disabilities, organizations for those who suffer anxiety & depression, are victims of mental and physical abuse and others. Your purchase and support helps to support these tremendously important causes.

Connect with me www.Elsewherewithyou.com

Gratitude & Thanks!